The Illustrated Rules of
ICE HOCKEY

By Tom Ayers
Illustrated by Eleanor Hoyt

Ideals Children's Books • Nashville, Tennessee

Dedicated to all the parents who get up at 4:00 A.M. and go to a cold rink to watch their children play hockey.
                                        —T.A.

For Mom, Dad, Sharon, Brian, Ann Marie, Christine, and for Craig.

With much appreciation to the Bridgewater Sports Arena, especially the Mighty Ducks League. Special thanks to my models Debi and Richard and to players Ross and Christopher for their time.
                                        —E.H.

Published by Ideals Children's Books
An imprint of Hambleton-Hill Publishing, Inc.
Nashville, Tennessee 37218

Printed and bound in the United States of America

Library of Congress Cataloging-in-Publication Data
Ayers, Tom.
    The illustrated rules of ice hockey / by Tom Ayers ; illustrated by Eleanor Hoyt.
        p.   cm.
    Summary: Provides general information about the game of hockey and about the specific rules of the game, and discusses the officials' signals, players' positions, and sportsmanship.
    ISBN 1-57102-048-9 (pbk)
    1. Hockey—Juvenile literature. 2. Hockey—Rules—Juvenile literature. [1. Hockey. 2. Hockey—Rules.] I. Hoyt, Eleanor, ill. II. Title.
GV847.25.A94   1995
796.962'02'022—dc20

                                                95-8068
                                                CIP
                                                AC

Table of Contents

Note to Parents:

This book offers an excellent way to capture and hold the interest of young ice hockey players, to give them information about important elements of the game, and to facilitate discussion of the game by players and their parents.

The rules in this book were written by an experienced hockey coach and were adapted from the "Official Playing Rules of USA Hockey, Inc.," a set of rules used by many youth hockey programs.

Parents can help a young player develop a strong interest in hockey by watching all the players on the ice and by being generous with compliments and encouragement. With positive attitudes and a good understanding of the rules of the game, everyone can enjoy the sport.

The Game of Ice Hockey

The game of ice hockey is one of the fastest team sports in the world. The speed and intense competition make it an exciting sport to play and to watch.

Ice hockey, as it is played today, has its roots in Canada. The first rules were borrowed from the Native American game lacrosse and were changed somewhat for playing on ice. The first formal hockey game was probably played in Montreal in 1875, by students from McGill University.

For a long time, U.S. hockey was played only in the northern states where there was plenty of outdoor ice for much of the year. As indoor rinks became more common, the popularity of the game spread. Ice hockey is now played in almost every state.

In 1910, ice hockey turned professional, and in 1917, the National Hockey League (NHL) was formed. Today the NHL has twenty-six professional teams, including eighteen in the United States.

The Stanley Cup, North America's oldest professional trophy, is the symbol of worldwide excellence in ice hockey.

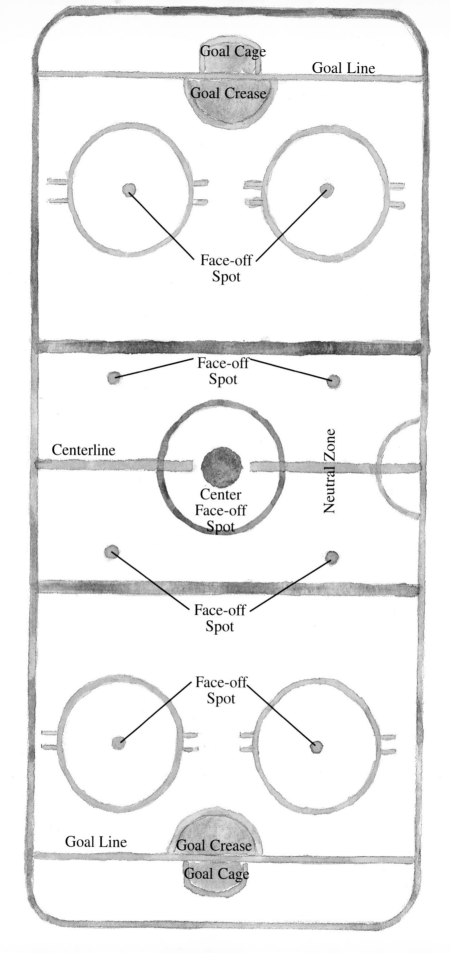

Goal Cage

Goal Line

Goal Crease

Face-off
Spot

Face-off
Spot

Centerline

Center
Face-off
Spot

Neutral Zone

Face-off
Spot

Face-off
Spot

Goal Line

Goal Crease

Goal Cage

The Rules of the Game

Rule 1: The Rink

The **rink** is the ice-covered surface on which ice hockey is played. It is usually 200 feet long and 85 feet wide and has rounded corners. A white wooden wall, called the **boards**, surrounds the rink. A clear plexiglass wall may extend above the boards.

The rink is divided by blue lines into three playing zones: defensive, offensive, and neutral. A team's **defensive zone** is the area in which the team works to prevent opponents from scoring a goal. A team's **offensive zone** is the area in which the team attempts to score a goal. One team's defensive zone is the other team's offensive zone. The **neutral zone** is the area between the blue lines.

At each end of the rink is a **goal line**. A **goal**, or **goal cage**, stands in the middle of each goal line (see Rule 9). In front of each goal is an area called the **goal crease**. The nine colored spots are called **face-off spots** (see Rule 11). Some rinks also have a red **centerline** which divides the rink in half. This area may also be called **center ice**.

Rule 2: The Stick

A hockey stick is usually made of wood from an ash tree. The wood is often covered with fiberglass. The blade of the stick may be no more than 12 $1/2$ inches long and 3 inches wide. Most blades are curved slightly in order to better control the puck. The stick itself may be no more than 60 inches long. For most youth players, the proper length hockey stick is one that extends from the ice surface to the player's chin while he or she is on skates.

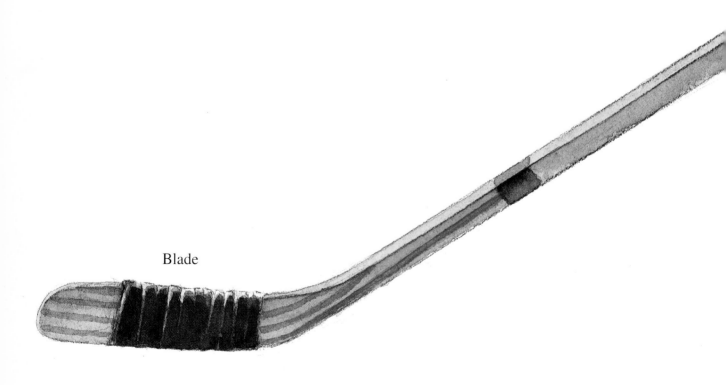

Blade

Rule 3: The Puck

The puck is a black disk made of hard rubber. It is 1 inch thick and 3 inches in diameter (the distance across the center). The puck must weigh between 5 1/2 and 6 ounces.

Before a game, the puck is frozen. This keeps it from bouncing on the ice during play. Several frozen pucks are kept near the rink, ready for when they are needed in the game.

Rule 4: Player's Equipment

The equipment that is used to protect a hockey player includes shin pads, gloves, shoulder pads, elbow pads, and a helmet with a face mask and mouthpiece. The shin pads, shoulder pads, and elbow pads are worn under the uniform. The helmet and face mask must be approved by the Hockey Equipment Certification Counsel (HECC).

The uniform should include padded pants with suspenders, stockings, and a sweater with the player's number on the back. The stick and skates should be checked for a proper fit. All equipment must be in good condition and worn with all straps fastened.

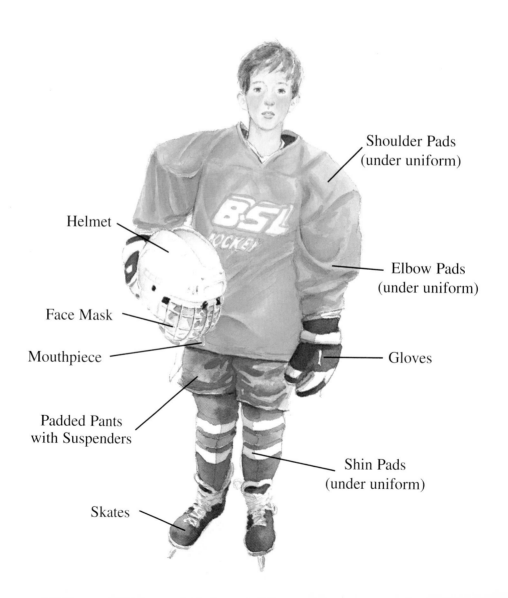

Shoulder Pads
(under uniform)

Helmet

Elbow Pads
(under uniform)

Face Mask

Mouthpiece

Gloves

Padded Pants
with Suspenders

Shin Pads
(under uniform)

Skates

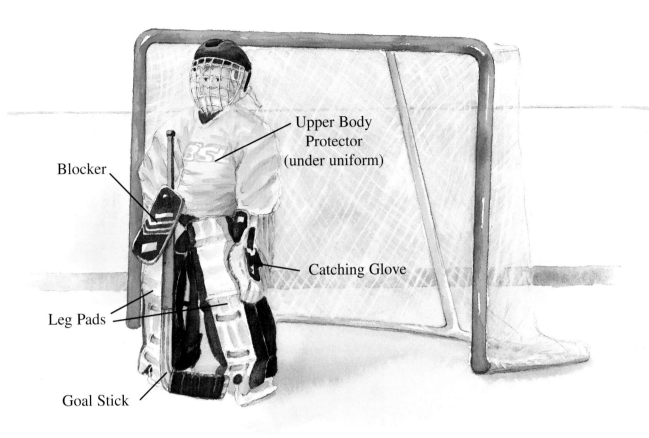

Upper Body
Protector
(under uniform)

Blocker

Catching Glove

Leg Pads

Goal Stick

The goalkeeper, or goalie, needs special equipment. This includes a catching glove, a blocker, an upper body protector, leg pads, and a goal stick.

Skates

Rule 5: The Team

Each team may have six players on the ice at a time. Three of these players are **forwards**: left wing, center, and right wing. Two are **defensemen**: left defense and right defense. The sixth player is the **goalkeeper**, or **goalie**. (See pages 22–27 for more information about players' positions.)

Rule 6: The Officials

In most games there are three officials on the ice. A **referee**, wearing red armbands, calls violations and penalties and determines if a goal has been scored. Two **linesmen** call off-sides and icing (see Rule 11), and they may assist the referee in calling violations and penalties. In some youth games, there are only two officials on the ice. Each performs the duties of referee and linesman. Other game officials are off the ice. They are: a **game timekeeper**, a **scorer**, a **penalty timekeeper**, and two **goal judges**.

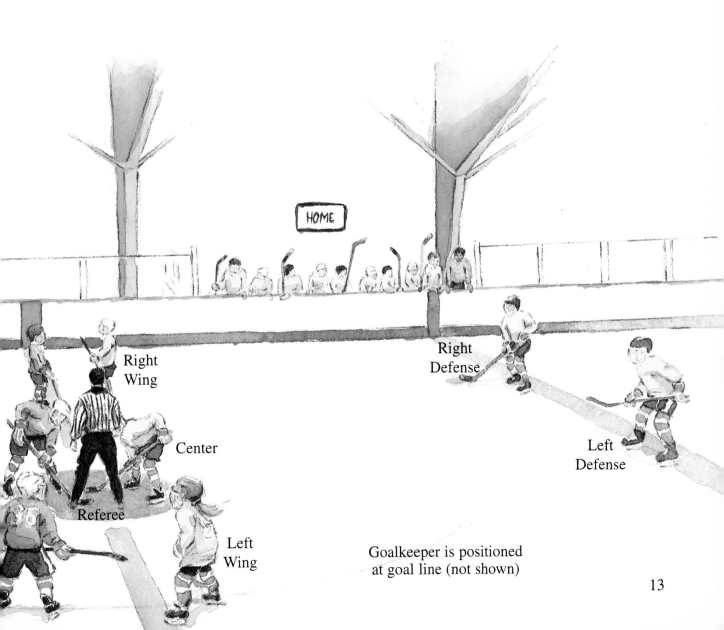

HOME

Right Wing

Right Defense

Center

Left Defense

Referee

Left Wing

Goalkeeper is positioned at goal line (not shown)

Rule 7: Duration of Game

The game of ice hockey is divided into three **periods**. Each period is no more than 20 minutes long, and there is a rest break between each period. The periods in a youth game are usually 10 to 15 minutes long. Each team may take one time-out during the game.

The game clock is stopped when an official on the ice blows a whistle, and it is started again when the puck is put back into play.

Rule 8: Substitution

A player may be substituted for any other player on the team at any time. Because a long time may pass before play is stopped, a change of players can take place "on the fly," that is, without stopping play and without reporting to an official.

Rule 9: Method of Scoring

A team scores a point, or a **goal**, when it sends the puck across the goal line and into the net or net area of the opposing team's goal. The entire puck must cross the goal line in order to score. If the puck is kicked or thrown into the net, it does not count as a goal.

The team with the most points at the end of the game is declared the winner. If the score is tied at the end of the game, a tie game may be declared, or the game may go into overtime if it is necessary to declare a winner.

Many organizations keep track of player statistics. One point is given to each player who scores a goal, and one point is given for each assist. An **assist** is credited to any player who handles the puck before the goal is made, as long as no more than two assists are counted for any one goal.

Net

Goal Line

17

Rule 10: Number of Players

A team may have no more than eighteen players, plus two goalkeepers. One player is chosen as **captain** and another as **alternate captain**. These two players act as spokespersons for the team, passing information between the referee and the coach.

Rule 11: Face-off

The start of each period begins with a **face-off** at center ice. For a face-off, one player from each team lines up so that they are facing each other. The referee drops the puck between them and play begins. A face-off at center ice is also used to start play after a goal is scored. A face-off at other locations on the ice occurs after one of the following violations.

1. **Off-side:** An offensive player crosses the blue line into the offensive zone before the puck goes into this zone.

2. **Icing:** A player shoots the puck from behind the red centerline over a part of the opponent's goal line that is not in front of the net. This is only called icing when both teams have an equal number of players on the ice.

Rule 12: Handling the Puck

Only the goalkeeper may use his or her hand to cover the puck and stop play. Other players may use their hands to pass the puck to a teammate only if both players are in their own defensive zone.

Rule 13: Puck Out-of-Bounds

If a puck leaves the playing area or strikes anything other than the boards, plexiglass, or an official, it is called **out-of-bounds**. A face-off (see Rule 11) is held in the place the puck was last played before going out-of-bounds.

Any time the referee loses sight of the puck, play is stopped and a face-off is held. The referee tells the players where to stand for the face-off.

Rule 14: Penalties

A **penalty** is called by the referee when a player or a team commits a **violation**, or breaks one of the rules. If a penalty is called against a player, that player must take a seat on the **penalty bench** or in the **penalty box**. That player's team will then play short-handed until the penalty time is completed. If a penalty is called against the team as a whole or against the team's goalkeeper, the penalty is served by one of the players who was on the ice at the time the rule was broken.

There are four kinds of penalties. A **minor penalty** means a player must sit for 2 minutes on the penalty bench; a **major penalty** means 5 minutes on the penalty bench; **misconduct** means 10 minutes on the penalty bench; and a **match penalty** means that the player may not play for the rest of the game.

One of the violations, tripping, is shown in the picture below. Other violations include charging, hooking, holding, interference, roughing, icing, elbowing, high-sticking, and cross-checking. Explanations of these violations and the officials' signals for them are shown on pages 28 and 29.

Rule 15: Penalty Shot

A player may be awarded a **penalty shot** if he or she misses a chance to score due to being fouled while in control of the puck in the offensive zone—if there is no defensive player between the player and the goalkeeper. A player may also be awarded a penalty shot if a defensive player intentionally covers the puck with a hand or other part of the body while the puck is in the goal crease.

When a player is awarded a penalty shot, the puck is placed at center ice. The player tries to score against the other team's goalkeeper while all other players are either off the ice or on the other side of the red line.

The Players

Ice hockey is a team sport in which each player's position is important. It is valuable for players to understand all the positions. Some players may even play different positions in different games. But during a game, each player should pay most attention to the job called for by his or her position. With practice, a player will learn to play his or her own position while being aware of what is happening in other positions.

Hockey is an interesting sport to play because it requires many different skills. One of the most important skills is the ability to skate well. Other skills are **stick handling**, **passing** the puck to other teammates, **shooting** the puck into the goal, and **checking** opponents by using the body or the stick to gain control of the puck. The more a player practices these skills, the better he or she will become.

The Forwards

There are three types of **forwards: left wing**, **center**, and **right wing**. The main job of these players is to score points. The forwards move the puck up the ice by passing it back and forth between themselves. They then try to get in a good position to take a shot at the goal.

Right Wing

Left Wing

Center

Forwards also play defensively by **back-checking** their opponents. This means they try to interrupt the other team's offensive **rush**, or attack.

Defenseman

The Defense

The two **defensemen** are called the **left defense** and **right defense**. They try to stop the opponent's attack at their own blue line. Defensemen block shots, clear the front of their goal, and body check forwards of the opposing team when they try to rush the net.

Defensemen also play offensively by taking the puck up the ice or by passing it to teammates who are forwards. Defensemen then follow the play into the offensive zone and help keep it there.

The Goalkeeper

The **goalkeeper**, or **goalie**, is the last line of defense. His or her main responsibility is to keep the puck from entering the goal. The goalkeeper may use the hockey stick or blocker to bat the puck away from the goal. The catching glove may be used to catch the puck and throw it away. The goalkeeper may also use his or her body to block shots.

Goalkeeper

27

Important Signals of the Game

Charging
Using one's body against an opponent at a very high speed or pushing the opponent from behind

Goal Scored

Holding
Using the hand, stick, or anything else to hinder an advancing opponent

High-Sticking
Carrying the stick at a level above shoulder height

Cross-Checking
Trying to stop an opponent by using a stick across his or her body

Penalty Shot

28

Roughing
Using unnecessary
force while playing

Elbowing
Extending an elbow
into an opponent

Hooking
Using the stick to hinder
an advancing opponent

Interference
Running into or hindering the
progress of an opponent who
does not have the puck

Tripping
Causing an opponent to fall by
interfering with his or her legs

Icing
Shooting the puck from behind the
centerline over a part of the
opponents' goal line that is not in
front of the goal

Sportsmanship in the Game of Ice Hockey

Ice hockey is one of the fastest team sports in the world. It is an intense and exciting game to play, and it allows body contact at high speeds. During a hockey game, the puck moves fast, players try to keep other players from touching the puck, and skates and sticks fly all around the ice. Because of the fast-paced nature of the game, good sportsmanship is essential. Fighting is never allowed, and a player who tries to injure another player is severely penalized.

An important part of showing good sportsmanship is playing together as a team. Players should help one another become star players by passing the puck and by putting their talents together. All should follow directions given by the coach.

Is winning important? Yes, it is, but it should not be the most important reason for playing the game of hockey. It is even more important to put forth your best efforts, to learn from others, and to learn from your own mistakes. When the game is over, it is a sign of good sportsmanship to say "Good game!" to the other team and to congratulate them on their playing skills—no matter which team has won.

Summary of the Rules of Ice Hockey

Rule 1: The Rink

The ice-covered surface on which ice hockey is played is called a rink. The rink is divided by blue lines into three playing zones: defensive, offensive, and neutral.

Rule 2: The Stick

A hockey stick is usually made of wood and covered with fiberglass. The blade may be no more than 12 1/2 inches long and 3 inches wide. The stick itself may be no more than 60 inches long.

Rule 3: The Puck

The puck is a black disk made of hard rubber. It is 1 inch thick and 3 inches in diameter (the distance across the center). The puck must weigh between 5 1/2 and 6 ounces.

Rule 4: Player's Equipment

The equipment includes shin pads, gloves, shoulder pads, padded pants, elbow pads, and a helmet with a face mask and mouthpiece. The goalkeeper's equipment includes a catching glove, a blocker, an upper body protector, goalie skates with protective shells, leg pads, and a goal stick.

Rule 5: The Team

Each team may have six players on the ice at a time. Three of these players are forwards: left wing, center, and right wing. Two are defensemen: left defense and right defense. The sixth player is the goalkeeper, or goalie.

Rule 6: The Officials

In most games there are three officials on the ice. A referee calls violations and penalties and determines if a goal has been scored. Two linesmen call off-sides and icing. Other game officials include a game timekeeper, scorer, penalty timekeeper, and two goal judges.

Rule 7: Duration of Game

The game is divided into three periods. Each period is no more than 20 minutes long, and there is a a rest break between each period.

Rule 8: Substitution

A player may be substituted for any other player on the team at any time.

Rule 9: Method of Scoring

A team scores a point, or a goal, when it sends the puck across the goal line into the net or net area of the opposing team's goal.

Rule 10: Number of Players

A team may have no more than eighteen players, plus two goalkeepers. One player is chosen as captain and another as alternate captain.

Rule 11: Face-off

The start of each period begins with a face-off at center ice. For a face-off, one player from each team lines up so that they are facing each other. The referee drops the puck between them and play begins.

Rule 12: Handling the Puck

Only the goalkeeper may use his or her hand to cover the puck and stop play. Other players may use their hands to pass the puck to a teammate only if they are both in their own defensive zone.

Rule 13: Puck Out-of-Bounds

If a puck leaves the playing area or strikes anything other than the boards, plexiglass, or an official, it is called out-of-bounds.

Rule 14: Penalties

A penalty is called by the referee when a player or a team commits a violation, or breaks one of the rules. There are four kinds of penalties: minor penalty, major penalty, misconduct, and match penalty.

Rule 15: Penalty Shot

A player may be awarded a penalty shot if he or she misses a chance to score due to being fouled while in control of the puck in the offensive zone. A player may also be awarded a penalty shot if a defensive player covers the puck with a hand or other part of the body while the puck is in the goal crease.

Vocabulary of the Game

body check: to bump the player who has the puck in an attempt to gain control of the puck

breakaway: a situation in which there is no defending player between the goalkeeper and the player with the puck

changing on the fly: substituting one player for another while the clock is running and the puck is still in play

freeze the puck: to hold the puck along the boards, causing play to stop

goal crease: the blue area in front of the net

hat trick: used to describe a player who scores three goals during one game

penalty bench (or penalty box): area in which a player serves time for a penalty

penalty killing: an attempt by a short-handed team to keep the other team from scoring by sending in players who are experts at back-checking

playmaker: a player who has three or more assists in one game

power play: when a team that has more players on the ice than the other team tries to score a goal

short-handed: describes a team that has fewer than six players on the ice due to penalties

stick check: to use one's stick to try to hook or poke the puck away from an opponent

violation: an action taken by a player or a team that breaks one of the rules